GUIDE TO AFFIRMATIVE ACTION
Revised

A Primer for Supervisors and Managers

Pamela J. Conrad
Robert B. Maddux

A FIFTY-MINUTE™ SERIES BOOK

CRISP PUBLICATIONS, INC.
Menlo Park, California

GUIDE TO AFFIRMATIVE ACTION
A Primer for Supervisors and Managers
Revised

Pamela J. Conrad
Robert B. Maddux

CREDITS:
Editor: **Michael G. Crisp**
Typesetting: **Interface Studio**
Cover Design: **Carol Harris**
Artwork: **Ralph Mapson**

Copyright © 1988, 1996 by Crisp Publications, Inc.
Printed in the United States of America.

Distribution to the U.S. Trade:

National Book Network, Inc.
4720 Boston Way
Lanham, MD 20706
1-800-462-6420

Library of Congress Catalog Card Number 96-85071
Conrad, Pam and Maddux, Robert B.
Guide to Affirmative Action—Revised
ISBN 1-56052-382-4

This book is printed on recyclable paper with soy ink.
PRINTED WITH SOY INK

LEARNING OBJECTIVES FOR:

GUIDE TO AFFIRMATIVE ACTION—REVISED EDITION

The objectives for *Guide to Affirmation Action—Revised Edition* are listed below. They have been developed to guide you, the reader, to the core issues covered in this book.

Objectives

- ☐ 1) **To explain Equal Employment Opportunity Commission (EEOC) legislation**

- ☐ 2) **To point out EEOC responsibilities of management to employees**

- ☐ 3) **To clarify management hiring and layoff responsibilities**

Assessing Your Progress

In addition to the Learning Objectives, *Guide to Affirmation Action—Revised Edition* includes a unique new **assessment tool*** which can be found at the back of this book. A twenty-five item, multiple choice/true-false questionnaire allows the reader to evaluate his or her comprehension of the subject matter covered. An answer sheet, with a chart matching the questions to the listed objectives, is also provided.

* Assessments should not be used in any selection process.

ABOUT THE AUTHORS

Robert Maddux

Robert Maddux is president of Maddux Associates, Consultants in Human Resource Management. He has consulted extensively with large corporations and small businesses over the past twenty years.

Mr. Maddux has designed and conducted management skills seminars in Canada, Europe and throughout the United States as well as consulting in the production of a number of management training films. He is the author of several best-selling management books including *Team Building: An Exercise in Leadership; Effective Performance Appraisals; Quality Interviewing; Successful Negotiation* and *Delegating for Results.* He is also the co-author of *Job Performance and Chemical Dependency;* and *Ethics in Business.*

Pamela Conrad

Experience in balancing a home and career spans over 30 years of parenting and 23 years in a corporate career. As a pre-school teacher Pam began to identify the needs of working parents and later as a Vice President in banking and Training Director in the credit card industry she was able to share her learning. Born and raised in Los Angeles, a DePaul University graduate, she currently resides in the Chicago area with her husband and two 83 year old in-laws; and is still balancing a home and career.

ABOUT THE SERIES

With over 200 titles in print, the acclaimed Crisp 50-Minute™ series presents self-paced learning at its easiest and best. These comprehensive self-study books for business or personal use are filled with exercises, activities, assessments, and case studies that capture your interest and increase your understanding.

Other Crisp products, based on the 50-Minute books, are available in a variety of learning style formats for both individual and group study, including audio, video, CD-ROM, and computer-based training.

CONTENTS

CONTENTS (continued)

PREFACE

As the second edition of this book goes to press, affirmative action programs have moved once again to the forefront of political and social debate, with leaders in Congress and the president calling for a review of federal programs and requirements. Whether or not these debates will lead to change remains to be seen but one thing is certain, the issues are many and they are increasingly complex.

When affirmative action was introduced in the 1960s, immigration was low, the population was predominantly white, and in most parts of the country African-Americans were the only minority group. But now, the population of the United States is vastly different. Racial and ethnic groups officially counted as "minorities" make up roughly one-third of the United States population—up from just over 10%. When women, who are included in most affirmative action programs, are added to the total, about two-thirds of the America population is eligible for some form of affirmative action.

Unless significant changes in legislation occur, managers must continue to establish, maintain and be able to demonstrate an organizational climate that assures all employees will be treated fairly and evaluated on the basis of their qualifications to perform the work assigned regardless of sex, age, race, religion or disability. Managers and supervisors must continue to be sensitive to their own prejudices and biases of others. They must weigh each personnel decision against job-related, objective criteria and conformance with the laws.

Those who turned a deaf ear to the legislative changes that have occurred since 1964, or thought this was an issue they could ignore, have learned a painful (and costly) lesson. The courts are filled with complaints of discrimination due to race, religion, sex, age, national origin, disability, or veteran's status. These complaints have already cost organizations hundreds of millions of dollars in fines and penalties, and it is likely the future will be even more severe. On a personal level, these charges have led to demotion, curtailment of promotion opportunities, loss of reputation and discharge for thousands of managers.

Until dramatic change occurs, this guide will continue to help managers recognize and understand equal opportunity and affirmative action and provide practical suggestions about how these challenges can be met.

Good Luck!

Pam Conrad

Robert B. Maddux

P A R T

1

Understanding the Problem and the Need

SELF-CHECK: UNDERSTANDING AFFIRMATIVE ACTION

Before you begin this book, take a few minutes to answer the following questions.

Yes   No

___ ___ 1. I understand the personal and organizational implications of discriminatory workplace practices.

___ ___ 2. I recognize factors in the workplace that might be construed to be illegal under existing equal employment opportunity (EEO) legislation.

___ ___ 3. I know how to correct conditions that could lead to complaints of discrimination.

___ ___ 4. I know how to test decisions against the requirements of EEO and affirmative action principles.

___ ___ 5. I communicate personal and organizational commitment to EEO and affirmative action principles.

___ ___ 6. I understand that equal opportunity is not just about gender or race, but also covers groups such as the disabled and people older than 40.

Have you checked any answers "no"? If you have, pay particular attention to the material in this book that will help you get to a "yes" answer. There are legal ramifications that could get you or your organization into serious trouble if you are uncertain about your obligations under the current laws.

4

EQUAL EMPLOYMENT OPPORTUNITY (EEO) LEGISLATION

Legislation since 1964 has had a dramatic impact on the workplace. New dimensions have been added to focus personnel decisions on bona fide job requirements and personal qualifications. Personal concerns about factors that do not have a direct bearing on the job are not considered. The emphasis of personnel laws has been on fairness and equity.

This EEO legislation has made subjective decisions costly for those who made them. Today all employees are eligible for recourse through a variety of legal channels if they feel their rights have been abused. This has forced management to re-think its decision-making criteria.

▶ What is true objectivity in making a personnel decision?

▶ What are the important and critical factors that *must* be considered?

▶ What is implied by the course of any action that is taken?

▶ Who will be affected and will they be affected for the right reasons?

▶ Where might subjectivity or bias slip in and supersede objectivity?

▶ How can this be minimized?

You can get a sense of the complexity of the issues involved by answering the questions on the next page.

TEST YOUR KNOWLEDGE

EXERCISE: Test Your Knowledge

Circle your answer, true or false, to the following questions. Turn to page 67 for the answers.

T (F) 1. Affirmative Action and Equal Employment Opportunity laws apply only to those doing business with the government.

T (F) 2. Affirmative Action is a quota system to ensure employment for a certain number of women and minorities.

(T) F 3. Minority and female applicants should not be hired or promoted if they don't have the qualifications necessary to perform the job.

T (F) 4. During an interview, a female applicant mentions she is divorced and has two small children. She qualifies for the position, but you are concerned about how the children will be cared for. In addition, you suspect she will be absent when the children are ill. These concerns will support a decision not to hire her.

(T) F 5. You must lay off one employee. You should select the one with the poorest performance record regardless of age, race, religion, sex, handicap or veterans status.

(T) F 6. A permanently disabled applicant who is confined to a wheel chair is technically qualified for a position in your data processing department. Hiring him would mean installing a ramp and modifying bathroom facilities for him. You should do it.

(T) F 7. As an employer, you are obligated to pay men and women equally for the job they perform regardless of any other income they may receive.

T (F) 8. Employees who tell ethnic jokes in their place of employment add to morale and good will and are therefore doing no harm.

T (F) 9. It is perfectly legal to ask applicants if they have ever been arrested.

(T) F 10. Any applicant or current employee has the right to bring charges against an employer for discrimination at any time.

SUMMARY OF FEDERAL EEO LAWS AND ORDERS

It is not necessary for all managers to understand and agree with every detail of these laws. It *is* important, however, that all managers understand the intent and spirit of the laws well enough to keep EEO considerations uppermost in their minds at all times. When unusual problems requiring in-depth knowledge arise, guidance can be obtained from those individuals in an organization specializing in the interpretation and application of these laws. If the organization is too small for such a specialist, top management may have to seek assistance from outside resources.

NOTE: The following represents only a summary of some major points of various EEO and affirmative action laws. Consult an expert for more in-depth information.

CIVIL RIGHTS ACT OF 1866 (42 USC 1981)

This law, known as section 1981, guarantees all persons the same right to make and enforce contracts that "white citizens" enjoy. It has been construed to cover virtually all private contractual arrangements including employment. Race is covered but sex and religion are not.

> **Example:** The courts, under section 1981 and Title VII of the Civil Rights Act of 1964, have held public officials, and in some cases private management members, personally responsible for damages in discrimination cases. (Faraca v. Clements, 506, F.2d 956 (5th Cir. 1975) Doski v. M. Goldsecker Co., 10 Fair Empl. Prac. Cas. 801 D. Md. 1975)

TITLE VII, CIVIL RIGHTS ACT OF 1964 (AS AMENDED BY EEO ACT, 1972)

Prohibits discrimination on the basis of color, race, religion, sex, or national origin. Covers all employers with 15 or more persons, all educational institutions, public and private, state and local governments, public and private agencies, labor unions with 15 or more members, joint labor-management committees for apprenticeship and training. Prohibits practices identified by statistically determined adverse impact as well as intentional unequal treatment.

Decisions concerning hiring, placement, training, promotion, termination and layoff are covered.

Title VII established the EEOC (Equal Employment Opportunity Commission) to enforce the law. The amendment in 1972 enables the EEOC to enforce Title VII through court action.

> **Example:** A TV station was ordered to pay $274,000 to a black newscaster who charged the station refused to promote him from weekend to weekday anchor because of his race. He claimed that after 10 years and more than 1200 broadcasts, white males with less training and experience were promoted. The court ruled it an act of discrimination because he was taken off the air for a month following his charges, followed by extensive documentation regarding errors in his performance. Refusing to give him a written contract similar to those given to whites was in violation of Title VII. (Lowery v. WMC-TV, Tennessee, 1987.)

EXECUTIVE ORDER 11246 (AS AMENDED BY EXECUTIVE ORDER 11375)

Requires an Affirmative Action Plan from all federal contractors and subcontractors that firms with contracts over $50,000 and 50 or more employees develop and implement written programs to be monitored by the Department of Labor. Revised order 4 covers underutilization of females and minorities and Rule 401:2741 covers payment of dues in private clubs that discriminate on the basis of race, sex, religion and national origin.

SUMMARY OF FEDERAL LAWS AND ORDERS (continued)

Executive order 11246 is enforced through compliance reviews during which the employer's Affirmative Action Compliance Plan and supporting EEO policies and practices are closely scrutinized.

EQUAL PAY ACT OF 1963

Requires that all employers subject to the Fair Labor Standards Act provide equal pay for men and women performing work substantially similar in skill, effort, responsibility, and working conditions unless wage differentials are due to bonafide systems of seniority, merit, output or some business factor other than sex.

OFCCP Enforcement

In 1965, President Lyndon Johnson signed Executive Order Number 11246, mandating employers with federal contracts to maintain written affirmative action plans.

The Office of Federal Contract Compliance Programs (OFCCP), an agency of the U.S. Department of Labor, administers and enforces the regulations of Executive Order 11246, which affects more than 200,000 employers.

The OFCCP keeps detailed records of the number of compliance reviews it conducts and the number of complaints the agency receives every year.

	FY 92	FY 93	FY 94
Compliance reviews	3,188	2,843	2,604
E.O. 11246 violation complaints	663	645	621
Complaints referred to EEOC	540	503	485
Total investigations completed	132	147	207
Violations of E.O. 11246	25	20	54
Debarments	2	1	5

Source: Employment Standards Administration, Office of Federal Contract Compliance Programs.

AGE DISCRIMINATION IN EMPLOYMENT ACT OF 1967

Prohibits employers of 20 or more persons from discriminating against persons between age 40 and 70 in any area of employment because of age. Some apprenticeship programs, retirement and/or benefit systems are excepted from these prohibitions. A number of states also have age laws and a few protect all ages. The subsequent Age Discrimination Act of 1975 prohibits discrimination on the basis of age against all persons 40 or older by any employer receiving Federal money.

Yes, we want to see all qualified applicants—we're an equal employment opportunity employer.

Example: The 3rd U.S. Circuit Court of Appeals affirmed a $652,000 jury verdict against Westinghouse Electric Corporation for willful violation of the Age Discrimination in Employment Act (ADEA). The case involved a senior engineer for Westinghouse who was terminated one month before his 64th birthday. The man, who had been employed for 36 years, was fired along with five other engineers whose ages averaged 5 years. The average age of engineers retained by Westinghouse after the layoff was 39.

The jury ultimately found that bias against older employees played a part in the decision to lay off the plaintiff and awarded him $267,000 in compensatory damages. The jury also determined that the violation was willful, which resulted in a double damages award which totaled $652,000, including attorney's fees. (Starceski vs. Westinghouse Electric Corp., No. 94-3182 and 9-3208 [3d Cir. 5/3/95].

SUMMARY OF FEDERAL LAWS AND ORDERS (continued)

NATIONAL LABOR RELATIONS ACT AND RELATED LAWS

Governs employers involved in interstate commerce and prohibits discrimination on the basis of race, national origin, sex, religion, and union activity or affiliation.

REHABILITATION ACT OF 1973 (As Amended)

This act is designed to promote the employment of handicapped individuals. It bans discrimination on the basis of visible and non-visible handicaps substantially limiting one or more major life activities. Further, companies must actively pursue opportunities to employ qualified handicapped individuals and modify their facilities to accommodate them.

Handicapped individuals are defined as persons who have a record of physical or mental impairment, history of alcoholism, asthma, diabetes, epilepsy and other diseases.

Example: Two female employees have applied for a position as Clerical Supervisor. The one who is the most experienced and the best qualified has recently had a mastectomy resulting from breast cancer. Because it requires five years to determine total cure, the other less qualified applicant is promoted. Since this is a step in the career path of a non-exempt clerical employee, the company didn't want to invest time and training in a person who might incur additional medical leave. Though an amendment to the Rehabilitation Act indicates that discrimination in the private sector is not illegal, persons who have a history of cancer are considered handicapped and cannot be discriminated against.

VIETNAM ERA VETERANS ACT OF 1974

Requires affirmative action in the hiring of qualified Vietnam-era veterans and disabled veterans for government contractors with any Federal contracts of $10,000 or more.

One key section of this act *requires* an employer, with a few exceptions, to list available job opportunities with the appropriate local state employment office nearest the facility where the opening exists.

PUBLIC LAW 103-353, THE VETERAN'S REEMPLOYMENT RIGHTS (VRR) LAW

The new 1994 statute expands the rights of servicemen and women who return to the workforce after a period of military service. The law broadly extends an employer's responsibility for providing COBRA coverage, increases the time that individuals can be away from the job and still maintain rights to reemployment, exposes employers to potential liability for service-related injuries, and expands the employer's responsibilities for making up contributions in pension plans. Regulations detailing compliance with the law may not be published for sometime, even though some of the law's provisions are already effective.

FREEDOM OF INFORMATION AND PRIVACY ACT OF 1974

Provides citizens with access to information on public officials and information compiled by the CIA and FBI. This act covers only government employees and provides them access to all information maintained and used in the hiring process, to grant salary increases and promotions and allows for such information to be contested or rebutted in a written document that must be maintained in the same file.

SUMMARY OF FEDERAL LAWS AND ORDERS (continued)

AMERICANS WITH DISABILITIES ACT OF 1990 (ADA)

The purpose of this act is to make it easier for disabled persons to hold jobs, travel, use public telecommunication services and integrate into society. The act prohibits discrimination based on disabilities in the areas of employment, public services, public transportation, public accommodations and telecommunications. Disabilities include visual, speech, hearing and orthopedic impairments, tuberculosis, HIV infection and AIDS, cerebral palsy, epilepsy, muscular dystrophies, multiple sclerosis, cancer, heart disease, diabetes, mental retardation and psychiatric disorders.

CIVIL RIGHTS ACT OF 1991 (CRA)

Amends Title VII, Civil Rights Act of 1964, Age Discrimination in Employment Act of 1967, and Americans with Disabilities Act of 1990. It creates the right to a jury trial and allows for recovery of compensation and punitive damages for intentional discrimination under Title VII. It encourages employers to establish and use a "grievance" or "open-door" policy to resolve problems before they become big. It addresses racial harassment on the job, the ability of employees to challenge discriminatory seniority systems, the rights of US citizens working outside the US, enforcement procedures under the Age Discrimination in Employment of 1967, and solutions under the Americans with Disabilities Act of 1990.

FAMILY AND MEDICAL LEAVE OF 1993 (FMLA)

Provides opportunities to balance the demands of the workplace with the needs of families. The Act is designed to permit eligible male and female employees to take up to 12 weeks of unpaid, job-protected leave within a 12 month period, for the birth, adoption or foster care of a child, to care for a sick child, spouse or parent who has a serious health condition, or for their own serious health condition.

ILLEGAL EMPLOYMENT PRACTICES

The following practices reflect the thrust of current legislation and the dangers inherent in careless personnel practices and techniques. Check ☑ those you need to learn more about. Then make sure you get the help you need.

Under Current Legislation It Is Unlawful To:

☐ 1. Refuse to consider for employment, or otherwise discriminate against, any person because of race, color, national origin, sex, religion, physical disability or age.

☐ 2. Show a bias in help-wanted advertising for or against applicants based on race, color, national origin, sex, religion or age unless you can prove your requirements are bona fide occupational qualifications.

☐ 3. Use any screening techniques for employment or promotion—paper and pencil tests, questionnaires—that cannot be proved to be directly job related.

☐ 4. Categorize job candidates on the basis of race, color, national origin, sex, religion or age.

☐ 5. Condone or permit sexual harassment of employees.

☐ 6. Segregate employees by race, religion, national origin with respect to working areas, toilet, locker, and/or recreational facilities.

☐ 7. Cause or attempt to cause an employer to discriminate against any person because of race, age, religion, national origin, sex, or veterans status through actions initiated by a union.

☐ 8. Refuse to hire a woman because separate facilities would have to provided. Nor can an employer refuse to hire a woman because the employer would have to pay her special benefits e.g., premium overtime, rest periods, etc. required by State law. (Note: An employer would have to give men the same benefits as women. Discrimination is a two-way street.)

☐ 9. Perpetuate past discriminatory practices that have led to statistical imbalances in the workforce.

☐ 10. Discharge, layoff, or otherwise terminate an employee on the basis of race, religion, sex, national origin or age.

14

Exercise: Identifying Minority Groups

"Minority" is a frequently used word in the language of equal opportunity. Do you know who is considered by law to be a minority? See how many minority groups you can identify in the list below. Circle any group that qualifies. Check your answers below.

1. Baptists
√2. Blacks
3. Obese people
④. White males
5. High school dropouts
√6. Chinese
√7. Vietnam veterans
8. Polish
√9. Men over 40
10. Jehovah's Witnesses
√11. Native Americans
√12. Married women
13. Jews
14. College students

15. Whites
16. Protestants
√17. Amputees
18. Teenagers
19. Single men
20. Smokers
√21. Hispanics
√22. Lesbians
23. Russians
√24. Blind people
√25. Women
√26. Homosexuals
√27. Filipinos
28. Catholics

ELEMENTS OF AN AFFIRMATIVE ACTION PLAN

It is likely your employer has developed an affirmative action plan (AAP) either because of legal requirements, or because of a voluntary commitment to assure equal opportunity for all employees and potential employees.

You may have participated in the preparation of an AAP directly and thus be familiar with its requirements. On the other hand, you may only be required to participate as a manager in the administration of such a plan. If the latter is the case, you should talk with those who developed the plan to determine specifically what it requires of you.

In general, an AAP is a detailed set of objectives and plans designed to achieve prompt and full utilization of minorities and women at all levels and in all areas of the covered work force. Affirmative action also includes providing job opportunities for the handicapped, disabled veterans and Vietnam-era veterans. Specific AAP objectives include to:

• Assign responsibility and authority for the program (and its progress) to a top company official.

• Establish a strong company policy and affirm commitment to equal employment opportunity.

• Identify jobs, departments and units where minorities and women are underutilized.

• Set specific, measurable, attainable hiring and promotion objectives with target completion dates in each area of underutilization.

• Reevaluate hiring criteria to ensure they reflect bona fide job requirements.

• Make legitimate efforts to find qualified women and minorities who can meet job requirements or become qualified to do so.

• Hold every manager and supervisor accountable for helping achieve the objectives of the AAP.

SAMPLE AFFIRMATIVE ACTION PLAN FORMATS

Following is a typical example of the format in which the mandatory elements of an affirmative action plan for women and minorities are expressed.

Compliance Plan for Women and Minorities

I. Title

II. Contents

III. Preface

IV. Equal Employment Opportunity Policy Statement

V. Distribution of EEO Policy Statements
—Internal
—External

VI. Designation of Responsibility for the Program and Its Implementation
—Identification, reponsibilities and authority of the EEO Administrator
—Responsibilities of management members

VII. Problem Areas
—Analysis of potential problem areas
—Corrective action

VIII. Development and Implementation of Action Programs

IX. Internal Audit and Reporting Requirements

X. Compliance with Sex Discrimination Guidelines

XI. Support of Community Action Programs

XII. How Minorities and Females Not Now in the Work Force Will Be Considered and the Establishment of Goals by Organizational Units

XIII. Discrimination Guidelines Relating to Religion and National Origin

XIV. Utilization Analysis
—Work force analysis
—Determination of job groups
—Availability analysis
—Determination of underutilization
—Goals and timetables

XV. Summary

Affirmative Action Plans for the Handicapped

Affirmative action plans for the handicapped and disabled veterans are similar to those for women and minorities. They do not, however, require establishment of goals and timetables, or a utilization analysis. The outreach, recruitment, and policy dissemination requirements are much the same.

AAPs for the handicapped must include the following:

▶ A policy statement signed by the chief executive officer (CEO) stating the company is committed to affirmative action for the handicapped and outlining affirmative action responsibilities for each executive, manager and supervisor.

▶ A statement on policy dissemination that should include all employees and union officials. The media, public and private recruitment sources, subcontractors, vendors and suppliers must also be notified of the policy and their support requested.

▶ Appointment of a member of top management to implement, direct and coordinate the plan.

▶ An internal auditing and reporting process to help monitor and measure progress in each aspect of the plan.

▶ A description of problem areas and the corrective action to be taken.

Affirmative Action Plans for Vietnam Era Veterans

The AAP for this group is normally integrated into other AAPs (such as women and minorities). It can be done separately however, using a format like the following.

    I. Preface
   II. Statement of Policy on Covered Veterans
  III. Responsibility for Affirmative Action
  IV. Implementation of the Plan
   V. Internal Review Procedures
  VI. Monitoring and Reporting

CASE STUDY #1: *The Promotional Opportunity*

Martin is manager of a department that has grown beyond expectations. He has been authorized to create a new supervisory position. The position requires five year's experience and offers opportunity for advancement.

Fred is 28 and has been with the company for four and one half years. He has worked in Martin's department the last two. He is married, has two small children and his wife is employed. Fred's work consistently meets standards. He is attending night school to complete his college education and has attended supervisory management classes. He feels ready for promotion and has applied for the new position.

Adele is 45. She has been employed 11 years. Divorced 12 years ago, Adele has raised two children who are now in college. She is ambitious and her performance exceeds standards. Because of her ability to organize and coordinate, she was appointed to chair the company picnic committee. By enlisting the help of all departments, she made the event a huge success. She has been promoted three times into higher clerical positions that took her to other departments. She has been in Martin's department three years and feels this, plus her broad knowledge of the way the company operates, qualifies her for promotion to supervisor. She has applied for the position.

Rick is 32 and has a degree in biology. He decided, after two years with a chemical company and five years as an insurance salesman, to try something else. He started to work in Martin's department one year ago. He has demonstrated his assertiveness and has developed several new ideas the company has implemented. Rick is single and enjoys sports and travel. His work exceeds standards, but his interpersonal skills have caused co-workers to avoid him. His "smart" remarks and know-it-all attitude make him difficult to work with but management regards him as a creative individual who can sell his ideas. The new supervisory position would give him the title and credibility he longs for, so he applied for the job.

Which applicant would you promote? Turn to page 69 for the authors' solution.

SEXUAL HARASSMENT

Title VII of the Civil Rights Act of 1964 prohibits sexual advances, requests for sexual favors, and other verbal or physical conduct of a sexual nature.

Sexual harassment charges can also be filed in state courts under tort laws. These cases often involve charges of intentional infliction of emotional distress, assault and battery or invasion of the right to privacy. These cases can be filed against *the supervisor or person* accused of the harassing *as well as the employer.*

Harassment Is Behavior of a Sexual Nature That Makes a Person Uncomfortable

- ✓ Men harass women
- ✓ Women harass men
- ✓ Homosexuals harass their own sex, or are harassed by members of the opposite sex

    (It is advantageous to address harassment of homosexuals, to protect them from discrimination and to be prepared for future legislation.)

On the next page, test your ability to identify sexual harassment.

20

EXERCISE: Test Your Ability to Recognize Sexual Harassment

Check any situation below that you feel would constitute sexual harassment.

☑ 1. A person has been made to feel that he/she must submit to or accept sexual overtures as a condition of employment.

☑ 2. A male allows his eyes to wander to a female's anatomy while having a conversation with her.

☑ 3. A person has been made to feel that to submit to or reject sexual conduct will affect his/her employment, advancement, evaluation, or work assignment.

☑ 4. A female worker's inappropriate attire causes an uncomfortable distraction among male co-workers.

☑ 5. Sexual conduct is intended to, or could possibly interfere with, the individual's work performance.

☑ 6. A person tells a joke about blondes, women or homosexuals.

☑ 7. An individual feels sexually intimidated by the work environment.

☑ 8. A female supervisor repeatedly invites a male subordinate to go out with her.

☑ 9. An employee, making a friendly gesture, touches another employee and causes discomfort or annoyance.

☑ 10. An employee makes an unwanted sexual advance to a person of the same sex.

☑ 11. Workers stare or whistle when a woman enters the workplace or a meeting.

☑ 12. Unwanted compliments about how clothing makes a person look.

ANSWERS: Any of the situations described COULD be sexual harassment. Some are considered harassment if there is only one occurrence. If a person's work performance is affected by repeated unwelcome gestures, actions, or language, harassment has taken place.

WHAT CONSTITUTES UNLAWFUL SEXUAL HARASSMENT?

In 1980 the EEOC identified the types of sexual harassment situations that could be construed to be unlawful discrimination. Subsequent court decisions have been generally consistent with these guidelines.

TYPES OF UNLAWFUL SEXUAL HARASSMENT	
Type	*Situation*
I	To be considered unlawful, three conditions must be met: 1. There must be verbal or physical conduct of a sexual nature. Usually this behavior is directed toward an applicant or an employee because of his or her sex. Examples include suggestive advances or requests for sexual favors. 2. The verbal or physical sexual conduct is *unwelcome*. The *unwelcome* behavior is usally persistent. 3. Acceptance or rejection of the sexual advances or requests becomes the basis of a decision affecting the person's employment.
II	Verbal or physical conduct of a sexual nature interferes with a person's performance. Such behavior often creates an offensive work environment for that person and they are intimidated by such conditions. Allowing sexually explicit language to flourish in the workplace, for instance, can lead to charges if any employee objects.
III	An employee receives an employment advantage—e.g., is hired, promoted, given more favorable hours than given other applicants or employees, because he or she sumitted to a sexual advance.
IV	A non-employee of the organization such as a customer, sexually harasses a company employee with the company's knowledge and the company does not take remedial action.

EXERCISE: My Attitude Toward Sexual Harassment

Before the serious effects of sexual harassment on individuals were acknowledged and legislation enacted to correct them, managers and supervisors often felt powerless to act or they "looked the other way." These attitudes supported the problem and often encouraged it. Some of these attitudes still prevail. Examine how you feel about sexual harassment by circling "agree" or "disagree" after reading each of the following statements.

1.	Whenever men and women work together, the man's role is to be dominant.	Agree	Disagree
2.	Sexual harassment never really occurs.	Agree	Disagree
3.	Women are overly sensitive to harmless male activities.	Agree	Disagree
4.	Women actually want men to be sexually aggressive toward them and that makes it alright if it is not intended to be offensive.	Agree	Disagree
5.	Women have been intimidated by men for years and it should stop.	Agree	Disagree
6.	Men are never sexually harassed.	Agree	Disagree
7.	Ensuring that a work environment is free from sexual harassment is the job of the supervisor.	Agree	Disagree

ANSWERS: If you agree with questions 5 and 7, you are ready to take positive action to prevent sexual harassment. If you agree with questions 1, 2, 3, 4, or 6, read the next page and take this quiz again.

SEXUAL HARASSMENT DOES EXIST

According to data collected by the Illinois Task Force at Sangamon State University, sexual harassment is being experienced by many individuals.

- 90% of all women surveyed think sexual harassment is a problem.
- 70% of all working women surveyed feel they have been harassed at one time or another.

Of those who felt they had been harassed:
- 52% had been subjected to sexual remarks or teasing.
- 41% had been the target of suggestive looks or leers.
- 26% had experienced subtle hints or pressure.
- 25% had been physically touched or grabbed.
- 20% had been propositioned.
- 14% had been repeatedly pressured to engage in a personal relationship.
- 9% reported other miscellaneous forms of unwanted sexual attention.
- 2% experienced forms of coercive sex.

TYPICAL FORMS OF HARASSMENT		
Verbal	*Visual*	*Physical*
Telling risque jokes Asking for sexual favors Comments about one's sexual anatomy Pursuing an unwanted relationship Unwanted compliments with sexual overtones	Wearing suggestive attire Staring at someone's sexual anatomy Flirting non-verbally Not wearing under-garments Sitting in a revealing position	Touching, making physical contact Standing too close A "too lengthy" handshake

VICTIMS OF SEXUAL HARASSMENT WILL:

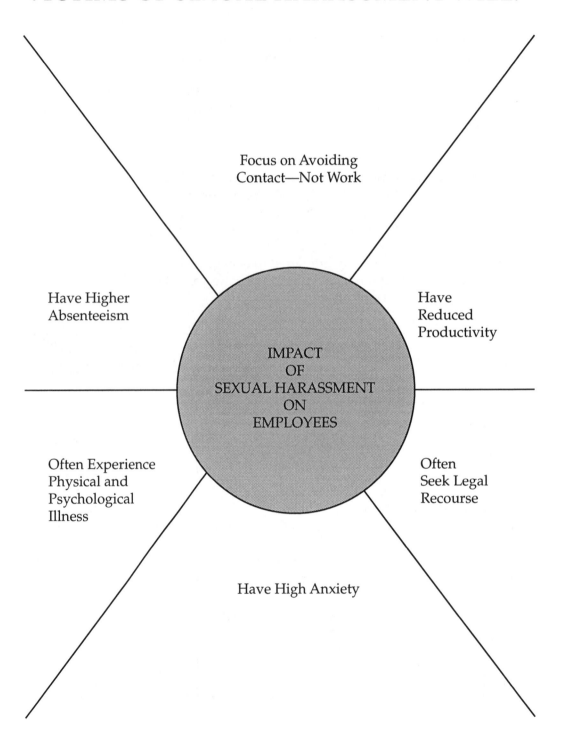

MANAGERS AND SUPERVISORS WHO DON'T COMPLY WITH THE LAW WILL:

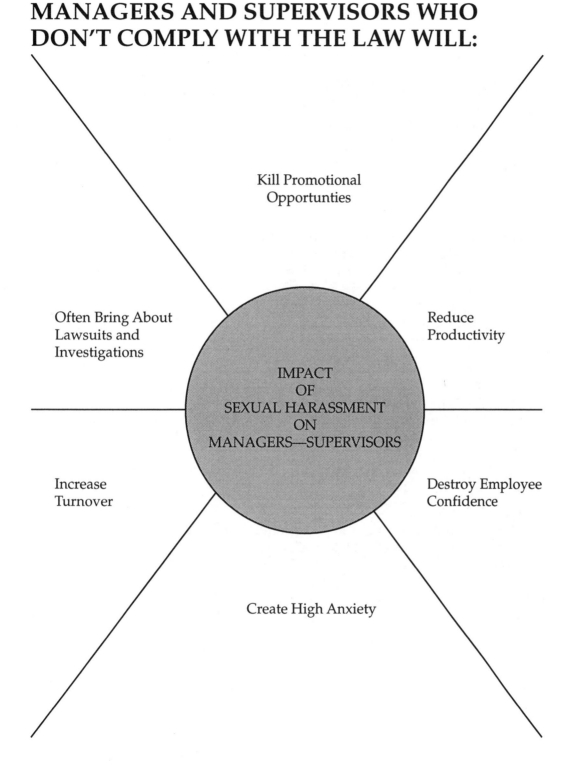

Kill Promotional
Opportunties

Often Bring About
Lawsuits and
Investigations

Reduce
Productivity

IMPACT
OF
SEXUAL HARASSMENT
ON
MANAGERS—SUPERVISORS

Increase
Turnover

Destroy Employee
Confidence

Create High Anxiety

CASE STUDY #2: *Sexual Harassment*

During her first two months of employment at Hercules Tire Company, Karen was still trying to cope with her new life as a divorced mother of two small children. Karen was 28 and had never held a permanent job outside her home prior to Hercules. She was trying to adjust to working in an industrial environment. Everybody, including her boss, seemed preoccupied with sex. Telling jokes, hanging cartoons in the lunch room, making comments to her about being single, suggesting drinks or dinner after work, and making comments about her clothes were common occurrences.

Karen has been dressing very conservatively to prevent any sexual attention. Recently, Sam Green, the General Manager and married father of three said, "Hi Babe, come into my office so I can show you how we do our month-end accounting." In his office, he said, "Wow, that dress really turns me on—you'd better be careful in the service areas 'cause those guys will love it." Karen was so embarrassed she almost missed his comment about her excellent work. He patted her on the rear and pulled a chair alongside his to begin working on the report.

Later, as she walked through the service area to get to the restroom, the workmen whistled and one offered his help if she needed it. Eileen Berk, her supervisor, found Karen in tears at her desk. Karen told her how embarrassed she was and of the anxiety she was experiencing because of the unwelcome attention. She also explained how important her job was. Eileen, an 18 year veteran, tried to explain that the men didn't mean any harm. They have always told dirty jokes during lunch and whistled at any girls who came around. Further, Mr. Green likes to have a pretty girl in the office because it is good for morale.

Karen has read some articles in magazines about sexual harassment. The descriptions of others who took legal action sounded like her situation. Karen, however, likes the work. It is close to home and the salary is good. She is reluctant to raise the issue with the Personnel department because she is afraid they won't believe her since she is relative newcomer or that Sam Green will seek revenge.

What would you recommend Karen do? Turn to page 69 for the authors' suggestions.

P A R T

2

The Employer's Role

ESTABLISHING THE GROUND RULES

Every employer covered by equal employment opportunity legislation has serious responsibilities to set, implement and enforce the policies, procedures and systems necessary for compliance with the law.

A strong policy statement from top management sets the tone and conveys the intent of the organization with respect to equal employment opportunity. The following policy statement is a representative example.

TO: *All Employees*
FROM: *Chief Executive Officer*

_____ *(Name of Company)* _____ *has been and will continue to be an equal opportunity employer. No employee or applicant for employment will be discriminated against because of race, color, religion, national origin, sex, handicap or veterans' status. We will take affirmative action to make sure applicaants and employees are treated without regard to these characteristics. To carry out our policy,*
_____ *(Name of Company)* _____ *will make sure that:*

- *persons are recruited, hired, trained and promoted for all jobs without regard to race, religion, age, national origin, sex, handicap or veterans' status.*
- *placement decisions are based solely on the individuals' qualifications in the positions being filled.*
- *other personnel actions, such as compensation, benefits, transfers, layoffs, returns from layoffs, company-sponsored training, education, tuition assistance, and social and recreation programs are administered without regard to race, religion, color, national origin, sex, or age.*

_____ *(Name of Company)* _____ *will periodically analyze its personnel actions to ensure compliance with this policy.*

Our EEO coordinator is _____ *(Name of Person)* _____ *, Executive Vice President. He / she is responsible for monitoring* _____ *(Name of Company)* _____ *'s affirmative action program. Contact this person if you believe you have not been treated in accordance with our policy.*

I ask your continued support and assistance in the fair and equitable administration of this policy.

Sincerely,

THE CEO

COMMUNICATING EEO POLICY

Organizations are required to communicate EEO policy both internally and externally. Some basic steps are shown below:

Internal Communication of EEO Policy

- Publicize commitment to EEO in organizational publications or other media using photographs including women, minorities, and the handicapped when appropriate.
- Conduct meetings with managers and supervisors to make clear the requirement that they take affirmative action to provide equal opporutnity in all personnel decisions.
- Inform managers and supervisors their equal opportunity efforts will be an ongoing part of their performance evaluations.
- Discuss the organization's EEO policy thoroughly in employee orientation meetings and in management development programs.
- Prominently post the organization's written EEO policy on bulletin boards.

External Communication of EEO Policy

- Inform all recruiting sources orally and in writing of company policy. Stipulate that these sources actively recruit and refer minorities and women for all positions listed.
- Communicate to prospective employees the existence of the organization's affirmative action program.
- Include women, minorities, and the handicapped in photographs used in any organizational publication including recruiting brochures.
- State the organization's equal employment opportunity status in all employment ads.
- Post all required state and federal posters concerning equal employment opportunity in conspicuous locations.

EXERCISE: Test Your Knowledge

How well do you know your organization's policy on EEO? To what extent are you held accountable for results? Test yourself by answering the questions listed below. If you are uncertain of any answer, clarify it with your supervisor or your Equal Opportunity Affairs Coordinator.

1. I have, or can find, a copy of my organization's EEO policy statement and affirmative action plan in _____

_____.

2. Our organization's EEO posters are prominently displayed in _____

_____.

3. My personal responsibility for EEO includes: _____

_____

_____

_____.

4. I have discussed the EEO policy of this organization with new employees at least _____ times this year, and with existing employees at least _____ times.

5. The EEO Coordinator for our organization is _____.
   His/her responsibilities include: _____

_____.

6. Disciplinary action for failing to adhere to and support EEO in this organization includes: _____

_____.

7. I spend approximately _____ hours per week anticipating and preventing discriminatory practices.

8. Areas of the organization's affirmative action plan that require action by me include: _____

_____.

ACTING AFFIRMATIVELY

The intent of an affirmative action program is to:
- Prepare a plan of action.
- Implement it.
- Follow through until the desired results are achieved.

The objective of an affirmative action plan is to ensure that equal opportunity exists for all current and prospective employees.

An Acceptable Affirmative Action Program Must Include:

✓ **An analysis** of the current workforce to determine the sex and race composition at each level.

✓ **Identification** of deficiencies in the utilization of minority groups and women.

✓ **Written goals** that include target areas where effort will be directed to correct the deficiencies.

✓ **Timetables** with specific dates by which to increase the utilization of minorities and women at all levels within the company.

✓ **Audit** processes that detail progress toward organizational goals.

Points to Remember

#1: Procedures, regardless of how well written, are meaningless unless meaningful effort is devoted to making them work.

#2: Effort that is undirected by specific and meaningful procedures is inadequate.

#3: Dedicated supervisors and managers who are committed to the success of affirmative action are what make the plan work!

DETERMINING UNDERUTILIZATION

The most important element in an effective affirmative action plan for women and minorities is an accurate utilization analysis. It involves analyzing all major job groups at a facility to determine if either women or minorities are being underutilized.

> *Underutilization Is Defined as Having Fewer Women Or Minorities in a Particular Job Group Than Would Reasonably Be Expected By Their Availability in the Job Market.*

A utilization analysis has these basic parts:

- Analysis of the workforce and its makeup in terms of classifications, wage rates, etc.

- Determination of job groups—similar in job content, wages and advancement opportunities.

- An availability analysis to determine the potential participation of women and minorities in particular job groups.

- Determination of areas of underutilization.

Supervisors and managers who actively participate in this process, or who make an effort to review the results, can readily see what is expected of them in terms of providing equal opportunity in the work groups they manage.

UNDERUTILIZATION FACTORS TO BE EVALUATED

To properly analyze the utilization of women and minorities, each group must be examined separately. The following criteria should be considered.

Underutilization of Women

▶ The number of unemployed women living in the area surrounding the facility.

▶ The percentage of females in the workforce as compared to the total potential workforce in the area surrounding the facility.

▶ The availability of women in the area with qualifying skills.

▶ Number of reasonably recruitable women with qualifying skills within the area surround the facility.

▶ Percentage of women looking for jobs in the area surrounding the facility or within a reasonable recruitment area.

▶ Number of promotable or transferable women within the organization.

▶ Percentage of women in training institutions in the labor area capable of training persons in needed skills.

▶ Ability of the employer to undertake training programs to develop women to qualify for all job classifications.

Underutilization of Minorities

▶ The minority population living in the area surrounding the facility.

▶ Number of unemployed minorities living in the labor area near the facility.

▶ Percentage of the minority workforce as compared to the total workforce in the surrounding area.

▶ Availability of minorities with the required skills in the immediate labor area.

▶ Number of reasonably recruitable minorities with the required skills.

▶ Availability of promotable or transferable minorities within the organization.

▶ Percentage of minorities in training institutions in the area providing training in the requisite skills.

▶ The ability of the employer to undertake training programs that would qualify unskilled minorities for all job classifications.

Myth or Reality: The White Male Advantage

Answer these questions about conditions within your organization.

❑ 1. All key decision makers are white males.

❑ 2. Management trainees are young, white males.

❑ 3. White males tend to associate exclusively with other white males.

❑ 4. White males get promoted more frequently than women or minorities.

❑ 5. White males have the advantage of better visibility by other white males in positions of power.

A ☑ answer to any of the above statements suggests white males may have a significant advantage in your organization—a violation of Title VII. What can you do to improve this?

ENFORCING EEO POLICY AND AFFIRMATIVE ACTION PLANS

Organizations must actively support and enforce EEO policies and affirmative action plans at all levels. This is best accomplished by:

1. Well defined and fully communicated EEO goals, policies, procedures and plans.

2. Measurable standards of performance for all levels of management with respect to every aspect of their EEO responsibilities. These should be part of each manager's written performance appraisal.

3. Current position descriptions and job specifications based on bona fide job requirements for all positions.

4. Fair, qualification-based hiring and promotional practices.

5. Periodic performance evaluation based on measurable goals and/or standards at all levels of the organization.

6. Disciplinary systems based on performance against standards and adhered to at all organizational levels.

7. Training of all personnel involved in the administration of EEO policy, the affirmative action plan and any phase of recruiting, hiring, compensating, training, promoting, disciplining, and laying off or discharging employees.

P A R T

3

The Role of
Managers and
Supervisors

EEO GUIDELINES FOR MANAGERS AND SUPERVISORS

You must protect the rights of your employees and your employer under current EEO legislation. The following guidelines suggest a positive way to do so.

▶ EEO legislation is complex and is constantly being tested and interpreted in the courts. Be alert for changes. When in doubt about how to proceed, seek the advice of your legal or equal opportunity affairs representatives.

▶ Create and maintain an atmosphere within your organization that demonstrates you are aware of and *support* equal opportunity policies.

▶ Refuse to permit discriminatory acts of any type by anyone in your unit. Racial slurs, jokes, and sexual harassment are offensive and have no place on the job. Even seemingly small incidents can make people *uncomfortable* and lead to charges of discrimination and subsequent investigations.

▶ Analyze the positions you supervise to ensure the qualifications required of the people who fill them are based on bona fide job requirements.

▶ Be sure non-discriminatory practices are being followed in all recruitment and hiring activities involving you.

▶ Look for possible inequities in pay, job assignments, special projects, training and promotional practices in your jurisdiction and correct them.

▶ Fully implement your company's affirmative action plans and, wherever possible, lend your expertise to their development.

▶ Make an effort to support and assist qualified females, minorities, and handicapped persons to advance within your organization.

▶ Document any disciplinary action you take. Also, carefully document your reasons for selection, termination, transfer, promotion or other personnel action. Be sure your documentation is adequate to support the action. If there is any doubt, check with a higher authority.

▶ Do not retain unsatisfactory performers for any reason. Make every reasonable effort to help them meet standards and document these efforts. Then, if they can't do the job, terminate them or move them to a position they can do adequately.

YOUR ATTITUDE TOWARD EEO IS IMPORTANT

If leaders do not place a high value on achieving EEO goals in their organization, the effort will fail. Success takes conscious effort to identify deficiencies and solve problems.

Poor or unreasonable attitudes about the abilities, habits, or likely behavior of females, members of racial or religious groups, and the handicapped, can destroy the will to accomplish EEO goals. It takes commitment to exert the effort required to maintain an appropriate work environment.

If you have not already done so, now is the time for you to begin to examine your attitudes and where they came from. What are you willing to do about them? (You can start the process on the next few pages.)

EXERCISE: Examine Your Attitudes About Women

Check the beliefs you agree with. Remember, honesty is the best policy. Compare your answers with those of the authors at the bottom of the page.

❑ Women have a higher turnover rate than men.

❑ Women are less capable than men.

❑ A woman's place is in the home.

❑ Every woman employee of child-bearing age will eventually take time off to have children.

❑ Working mothers always need time off when children are sick.

❑ Women will not devote as many hours to a career as men.

❑ Married women take jobs away from men who are the sole support of their families.

❑ Women should stick to women's jobs.

❑ Women don't want responsibility.

❑ Women tend to bring their "home" problems to work with them.

❑ Men don't like to work for women.

❑ Women simply can't compete at executive levels.

❑ Women don't need as much salary as men.

❑ Women are too emotional to make good decisions.

If you agree with any of these statements, you may be on your way to a Title VII violation.

ATTITUDES AFFECT BEHAVIOR

Our attitudes are reflected in our behavior. They usually govern our actions and determine our sense of direction. Sometimes we are fully aware of this. At other times we are not.

▶ *If our attitudes contain bias and prejudice, there is a very good chance these will be reflected in our work ethic and business decisions.*

▶ *The end result may be an inability to deal positively with some major human issues on the job.*

▶ *If you feel this could be happening in your case, do something about it. Education, gathering facts, examining your attitude toward women and minorities and realistic evaluation of the issues may be required.*

ALWAYS REMEMBER:

YOU ARE RESPONSIBLE FOR YOUR ATTITUDES AND BEHAVIOR!

EXERCISE: Examine Your Attitude Toward Minorities

Check the beliefs you agree with, then check your answers with those of the authors at the bottom of the page.

❑ Anyone with a physical handicap is unable to produce as much as those who are not handicapped.

❑ Racial minority employees will not be accepted by the organization's customers.

❑ People practicing certain religions are unable to work weekends.

❑ People without a high school diploma cannot read, alphabetize, or calculate.

❑ Anyone who has been arrested will probably cause problems as an employee.

❑ A person's medical history will indicate how well they will produce in the future.

❑ White people are more intelligent and experienced than blacks and Hispanics.

❑ Minority employees will cause uprisings or racial protest demonstrations.

❑ Minorities don't need as much salary as whites.

❑ Minorities who don't speak English well will not be able to follow or give directions.

❑ Older people approaching retirement cannot be considered stable employees.

❑ Veterans receiving disability payments can get by on lower salaries and fewer benefits.

If you agree with any of these statements, you could be headed for trouble either legally or interpersonally. It would be a good idea to check the facts to ensure compliance with federal or state laws.

SIGNS OF DISCRIMINATION

As a manager or supervisor, you have an obligation to identify potential areas of discrimination or harassment and then act as a role model by using appropriate language and displaying behavior that supports equal opportunity and affirmative action.

To effectively support EEO guidelines, you must develop an awareness of the signals that tell you discrimination it taking place. This may go against your personal value system. If it does, educate yourself about the law and the possible consequences of violation. It will help you see reasons why you must adopt a positive attitude toward EEO in your leadership style.

It is increasingly essential to take an active rather than a passive role to discourage discrimination and to support policies and procedures. For good reasons, EEO is here to stay!

**This is not the way to approach
any kind of discrimination!**

EXERCISE: Stay Alert for Signs of Discrimination

It is important to recognize signals that suggest discrimination. Ignoring subtle indicators of discriminatory practices can lead to BIG problems.

Following are signals that suggest discrimination is taking place. Put a check in front of any you know exist in your organization. Then set up an action plan to correct the discrimination practice.

❑ Personnel are segregated

❑ There is no formal statement of EEO policy

❑ Ethnic jokes are told in public and not discouraged by management

❑ Women are poorly represented in management positions

❑ Minorities are poorly represented in management positions

❑ Employees are encouraged to attend "all male" or all "minority" meetings and functions

❑ Women and minority applicants are declined positions more frequently than men and non-minorities

❑ Opportunities for career improvement are not routinely offered to women and minorities

❑ Men and women are paid different salaries for comparable work

❑ There are few minority employees

❑ There is a significant lack of employees over 40

❑ There is no written affirmative action plan

❑ An affirmative action plan exists but managers and supervisors have not been trained in awareness or compliance

❑ Provisions for the handicapped do not exist at entrances, in rest rooms or in parking lots

❑ Women are treated differently than men in most aspects of the work

❑ Minorities are positioned in the lower paying jobs

❑ Management's attitude is that sexual harassment is brought on by the one harassed or that it does not exist

PERPETUATING DISCRIMINATION

Perpetuating discrimination is something you may be doing unconsciously.
Usually it is based on your personal values, or the way your role models operate,
or merely because that is the way things have always been done.

Your values were set early in life. They were influenced by your parents,
teachers, local politics, the economy, music, religious influence, scientific
discoveries and many other elements that played a role in your life.

▶ When you assign a project to a member of your staff,
question whether you may be discriminating.

▶ The way that you develop—or neglect to develop—your
staff for promotional opportunities may be discriminatory.

▶ How you hire, promote, fire, or select candidates for layoff
may be violations of EEO laws.

**TO CONTINUE PRACTICES THAT PERPETUATE
DISCRIMINATION IS ILLEGAL
WHETHER DONE CONSCIOUSLY OR UNCONSCIOUSLY!**

EXERCISE: Do Not Perpetuate Discrimination

Any time a manager or supervisor makes a decision involving employees, he or she has an opportunity either to discriminate against them or to support equal opportunity.

Put a check in front of any practice you feel perpetuates discrimination in any organization. Then check your responses with those of the authors at the bottom of the page.

1. ___ Refusing to hire a pregnant woman because she may elect to stay home after the birth

2. ___ Not scheduling older workers for training because it would be a waste of time and money

3. ___ Giving a handicapped individual special consideration in meeting production goals

4. ___ Eliminating qualified persons from consideration for a job due to lack of formal education when education is not a job requirement

5. ___ Hiring qualified minority applicants regardless of the personal bias of customers

6. ___ Allowing an employee time off for religious activities, or allowing religious practices on company time so long as it doesn't affect production

7. ___ Judging candidates for hire or promotion by including more than just their ability to perform the job

8. ___ Selecting an employee for a project should be focused on the top performers

9. ___ Identifying candidates for layoff should never include minorities

10. ___ Promoting young men within the company will ensure stable and consistent management in the future

ANSWERS: Following the practices outlined in 1, 2, 3, 4, 7, 9 and 10 can lead to serious problems and will certainly support discrimination.

Guide to Affirmative Action

DETERMINING JOB REQUIREMENTS OBJECTIVELY

Bona fide job requirements for each position you manage is fundamental for sound recruiting and selection procedures. The same is true for evaluating and compensating performance, selecting employees for training, promotion, layoff and/or discharge.

Each position under your supervision should be reviewed periodically to be sure the job specifications and requirements are current and accurate. The significant considerations in this process are outlined on the following page.

CURRENT JOB REQUIREMENTS AND SPECIFICATIONS THAT ARE OBJECTIVELY DERIVED FACILITATE ADHERENCE TO EEO LAWS AND THE ACHIEVEMENT OF AFFIRMATIVE ACTION PLANS.

CHECKLIST: How to Determine Job Requirements

Information about jobs falls into five basic categories and can be gathered accordingly.

#1 THE PURPOSE OF THE JOB:
- ❏ What is the ultimate product or service desired?
- ❏ What is the relationship of the job to others in the organization?
- ❏ What are the consequences of poor or non-performance?

#2 WHAT THE JOB HOLDER ACTUALLY DOES:
- ❏ What are the most important duties performed?
- ❏ What are the secondary duties?
- ❏ How often are the duties performed?
- ❏ What is the nature and scope of decision making?

#3 HOW THE PERSON PERFORMS THE JOB:
- ❏ What are the reporting relationships?
- ❏ What internal and external contacts are involved?
- ❏ What are the general working conditions (e.g., place, hours, hazards, advantages, co-workers)?

#4 WHAT HUMAN RELATIONS AND PERSONAL SKILLS ARE REQUIRED:
- ❏ What interpersonal skills are required to support relationships with others?
- ❏ Is the position detail-oriented?
- ❏ Is logic or reasoning required?
- ❏ What specific skills are absolutely essential?
- ❏ Is good grooming required?
- ❏ How important is attitude?

#5 WHAT PHYSICAL ATTRIBUTES ARE NECESSARY:
- ❏ Is physical strength required?
- ❏ Is body size a factor?

NOTE: Job placement based on physical attributes must be legitimate. If you elect not to hire a handicapped person, you may be required to show:
- ✓ *Specifically how the handicap prevents the person from doing the work.*
- ✓ *How the person would create a health or safety hazard for others.*

MAKE RATIONAL DECISIONS ABOUT PEOPLE

Managers and supervisors are required to make many decisions about people. They make these decisions as they select, assign, train, compensate, promote, evaluate, and/or terminate employees.

Everyone has certain prejudices. Leaders must recognize theirs and neutralize them during the decision-making process. It is essential, while making personnel decisions to:

▶ Evaluate all applicants or persons in the same positions by using the same performance-based criteria.

▶ Be aware of the organization's EEO goals.

▶ Respect Federal, State or local laws regarding EEO.

▶ Give all persons the same opportunity considerations.

One method of comparing job applicants for a given position is shown on the next page.* Similar methods can be used to increase objectivity in making other personnel decisions.

HOW NOT TO SELECT, ASSIGN, TRAIN, COMPENSATE, PROMOTE, EVALUATE AND/OR TERMINATE EMPLOYEES

---

*For a complete review of the selection process order *Quality Interviewing* by Robert Maddux, Crisp Publications: Menlo Park, CA.

Comparison of Candidates to Position Requirements

POSITION TO BE FILLED: <u>**Administrator/Community Health Education**</u>

Rate each candidate using the following scale.

1. Knowledge and/or skill level well below position requirements.
2. Knowledge and/or skill level meet minimum position requirements.
3. Knowledge and/or skill level meet all position requirements.
4. Knowledge and/or skill level unusually extensive and useful in this position.
5. Knowledge and/or skill level exceed position requirements.

Circle the name of the candidate selected.

Requirements	CANDIDATES			
	S. G. *Jerome*	*P. R.* *Parker*	*N. S.* *Sherman*	*A. P.* *Norman*
	RANKING			
General Knowledge:				
1. *Community Health Education Functions*	1	2	4	2
2. *Personal computers*	3	2	3	2
3. *MicroSoft Word*	3	2	4	3
4. *Excel*	3	2	3	3
Specific Job Skills and/or Knowledge:				
1. *Typing—55 wpm*	3	3	3	3
2. *Spelling & Grammar*	2	3	3	3
3. *Basic Math Skills*	1	3	4	2
4. *Page Layout*	3	3	4	3
Administrative Skills and/or Knowledge:				
1. *Filing & Filing Systems*	2	3	4	3
2. *Office Machines*	2	3	3	3
3. *Office Procedure & Practice*	2	3	4	3
Attitude	3	3	4	4
TOTALS	28	32	43	34

MINIMIZE DISCRIMINATION IN EVALUATING PERFORMANCE

Discrimination is frequently charged when decisions involving promotion, compensation, assignment to projects, selection for training, probation and discharge are based on seemingly subjective criteria.

Supervisors and managers will reduce their vulnerability to criticism and charges of bias when they measure performance against previously and mutually set performance expectations.* These expectations, frequently referred to as goals and standards, are described on the next page.

*For a complete review of the performance appraisal process order *Effective Performance Appraisals* by Robert Maddux, Crisp Publications: Menlo Park, CA.

USING GOALS AND STANDARDS TO MEASURE PERFORMANCE

The appraisal process starts when the employee and supervisor reach a mutual understanding of what needs to be accomplished. If expectations are not clearly stated, mutually understood and presented in measurable terms, performance will be difficult to evaluate.

Goals and standards are methods by which job expectations can be expressed. Those responsible for performance appraisals need a good understanding of goals and standards, and how to use them during the appraisal process.

GOALS

*A **goal** is a statement of results which are to be achieved.* Goals describe:

• Conditions that will exist when the desired outcome has been accomplished

• A time frame during which the outcome is to be completed

• Resources the organization is willing to commit to achieve the desired result.

Goals should be challenging, but achievable and established with the participation of those responsible for meeting them. Here is an example:

To increase the flow of invoices through the Accounting Department to a minimum of 150 per day by October 1. The total cost increase to accomplish this should not exceed $550.

Once accomplished, a new goal can be established to emphasize the next set of desired results.

STANDARDS

*A **standard** refers to an ongoing performance criteria that must be met time and time again.* Standards are usually expressed quantitatively, and refer to such things as attendance, breakage, manufacturing tolerances, production rates and safety standards. They are the most effective when established with the participation of those who must meet them. Here is an example:

The departmental filing backlog should not exceed one week. Any record requested should be available within five minutes of the request.

In general, goals apply more to managers and professional employees who engage in individualized projects. Standards are more common for workers engaged in routine, repetitive tasks.

AVOID CHARGES OF BIAS WHEN CORRECTING PERFORMANCE

Experts believe at least 50% of all performance problems in business occur because of a lack of feedback. An employee will see no reason to change his or her performance if it appears acceptable to the supervisor and the organization. If there is a problem, it will continue if it is not communicated to the employee.

Many managers and supervisors do not take corrective action when it should be done because they do not know how, or fear negative consequences (including charges of bias and discrimination) if they do. Corrective action can be taken positively, however, by proper preparation, planning, and discussion with the employee.

Complete the following case study and then read on to briefly review some of the essential techniques to help you take corrective action when unsatisfactory performance occurs.

CASE STUDY #3: *The Discharge That Backfired*

Reuben has been working as a billing clerk under the supervision of Bill Williams for about two years. Bill supervises a group of eight. Each employee performs similar duties with experience ranging from six months to four years. Bill provided the initial training for each employee, but did not set any kind of standards by which their performance could be measured objectively. Performance reviews are not required by the company and Bill has never considered doing any on his own.

Errors frequently occur but Bill has not done much about them. He usually just sends them back for correction saying, "Please do better next time." He recently came to the conclusion however the Reuben was making more errors than anyone else. Bill decided to fire Reuben to make a point with the others.

Reuben, the only black in the group, was dumbfounded. He couldn't see that his error rate was worse than anyone elses. Consequently, he assumed he was being discriminated against and filed charges.

In the space below, please indicate how you would have supervised this group and handled this situation.

What you would have done differently:

_____
_____
_____
_____
_____
_____
_____

Now turn to page 71 for the authors' suggestions.

Supervisors and managers who avoid performance appraisals—or put them off to the last minute—do the employee, the company and themselves a disservice.

The material on the next page will help you chart a safe course for your next appraisal session.

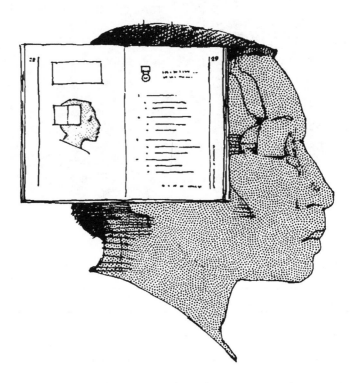

Thorough preparation is required if correction of a performance problem is to occur. This same preparation can prevent any possibility of bias and a subsequent judgment of discrimination.

MANAGERIAL PREPARATION
FOR PERFORMANCE APPRAISALS

Prior to conducting a performance appraisal, identify and develop all items that need to be covered. Since employee performance in the current job is the central issue, gather relevant data concerning job requirements and established goals or standards. Then, assess the employee's performance on the above for the appraisal period. For effective performance appraisals it is essential to:

#1 Review the job description or requirements to be sure your knowledge is current.

#2 Review the goals and standards previously discussed and agreed upon with the employee plus any documentation you have relating to their achievement.

#3 Review the employee's history including:
- job skills
- training
- experience
- special or unique qualifications
- past jobs and job performance

#4 Evaluate the actual job performance versus job expectations for the period being appraised.

#5 Note any variances in the employee's performance that need to be discussed. Provide specific documented examples of excellent or poor performance.

#6 Consider promotable possibilities and career opportunities for this person. Be prepared to discuss them.

When the personal appraisal focuses on job expectations previously agreed upon with the employee, and how well they have been accomplished, it is hard to say discrimination is at work.

The checklist on the next page will help you plan a well-balanced dialog in an atmosphere conducive to creating a constructive solution to a performance problem.

▶ A well-conducted performance appraisal discussion will prevent misunderstandings and charges of bias or discrimination.

▶ A well-constructed performance discussion makes it very apparent to the employee that performance is the issue—not some bias or prejudice.

Carefully documented examples of any problem, and the long-term implications of this problem for the employee and the organization, will provide the foundation upon which a discussion plan can be built.

CHECKLIST AHEAD

CHECKLIST: Plan the Appraisal Discussion

Use this checklist when planning performance or problem-solving discussions with your employees.

#1 CREATE A SINCERE, OPEN AND FRIENDLY ATMOSPHERE.
- ❑ Review the purpose of the discussion.
- ❑ Make it clear it is a joint discussion and the employee's views and ideas are expected.
- ❑ Strive to put the employee at ease.
- ❑ Listen.*

#2 KEEP THE FOCUS ON JOB PERFORMANCE AND RELATED FACTORS.
- ❑ Discuss job requirements, employee strengths, and specific improvement needs.
- ❑ Be prepared to cite specific examples for each point discussed.
- ❑ Encourage the employee to assess his/her own performance on issues being discussed.
- ❑ Use open, reflective and directive questions to promote thinking, understanding and problem solving.
- ❑ Listen.*

#3 ENCOURAGE THE EMPLOYEE TO COME UP WITH HIS OR HER OWN IMPROVEMENT PLANS.
- ❑ Try to get the employee to set his/her own improvement targets and goals, and reinforce positive contributions.
- ❑ Agree on an action plan that specifies what the employee intends to do, and a timetable for doing it.
- ❑ Listen.*

Anticipating what the employee's reaction will be to the discussion often provides valuable insights into successful ways to conduct the session.

---

*For a book that covers this topic in more depth, order *The Business of Listening* by Diane Bone, Crisp Publications.

TEN UNFORGIVABLE MISTAKES

Behaviors that perpetuate discrimination, harassment or unfair treatment must be avoided if we are to succeed in providing equal employement opportunities and practices in this country. Managers and supervisors must look at their own behaviors—as well as those of employees—that are inappropriate and lead to unfair teatment.

Check the behaviors that you feel need to change in your company.

❑ Ignoring employees who discriminate or harass knowingly or unknowingly.

❑ Considering ethnic joke telling as harmless fun.

❑ Selecting individuals for employment, promotion, layoff, or projects based on personal preferences instead of job requirements.

❑ Neglecting opportunities to train women and minorities to become promotable.

❑ Asking questions about age, high school or college completion dates, marital status or family obligations during pre-employment interviews.

❑ Creating a project team, task force, or management group that excludes women or minorities.

❑ Continuing to pay different salaries to men and women in the same job description with equal qualifications and/or experience.

❑ Allowing pictures of scantily clad women in the workplace.

❑ Eating lunch only with other managers and supervisors or other activities that create a perception that management should not mingle with line workers.

❑ Failing to provide training for managers and supervisors so that they are not in compliance with equal employment opportunity laws.

EXERCISE: Reading Review

Answer the following true/false questions. Check your answers on page 68.

T	F
	✓
	✓
	✓
✓	
✓	
✓	
✓	
	✓
✓	
	✓
✓	
✓	
	✓
✓	
	✓

1. EEO laws are unjustified.
2. Women have always been paid what they are worth in comparison to men.
3. Minorities have vivid imaginations, which leads them to believe they are discriminated against.
4. Title VII, Civil Rights Act of 1964 prohibits discrimination on the basis of color, race, religion, sex or national origin.
5. Persons between the ages of 40 and 70 are protected by the Age Discrimination in Employment Act of 1967.
6. Handicapped individuals are defined as persons who have a record of physical or mental impairment, history of alcoholism, asthma, diabetes, epilepsy or other disease.
7. The 1980 Sexual Harassment Guidelines provide that an employer is responsible for the acts of its agents and supervisory employees with respect to sexual harassment.
8. It is O.K. to use paper and pencil tests to screen applicants if you feel these instruments help you make a hiring decision.
9. The Family and Medical Leave Act of 1993 (FMLA) allows fathers to take family care absence for the birth of a baby.
10. According to the Americans with Disability Act, an employer should disqualify an applicant who requires special equipment, furniture, or workspace needs.
11. Affirmative action includes seeking job opportunities for the handicapped, disabled veterans and Vietnam-era veterans.
12. It is possible that sexual harassment charges can be filed against the supervisor or person accused of the harassing as well as the employer.
13. There is little the supervisor can do to promote equal employment opportunity.
14. Performance-based decision making is essential when handling personnel matters.
15. EEO legislation is well accepted and adhered to in today's business environment.

DEVELOP A PERSONAL ACTION PLAN

> *Reflect for a moment on what you have been learning—then develop an action plan to apply these concepts. The guide on the next page may help.*

Think about the material you have read. Review the self-analysis questionnaires. Re-think the case studies and the reinforcement exercises.

What have you learned about equal employment opportunity applications?

_____

_____

_____

_____

_____

_____

What did you learn about yourself? Make a commitment to yourself to become more effective by designing a personal action plan to help you deal with any equal employment opportunity problems you encounter.

_____

_____

_____

_____

_____

_____

The guide to a personal action plan on the next page can help you clarify your goals and outline actions required to achieve your goals.

MY PERSONAL ACTION PLAN

1. My current knowledge of equal employment opportunity laws and the company's affirmative action plan is.

    ADEQUATE _____   NEEDS IMPROVEMENT _____

2. I need to improve my knowledge and understanding in the following areas.

    _____

    _____

    _____

3. My goals for improving the status of my organization under the company's affirmative action plan are as follows. (Be sure they are specific, attainable and measurable.)

    _____

    _____

    _____

4. The following people and resources can help me achieve my goals.

    _____

    _____

    _____

5. Following are my action steps along with a timetable to accomplish each goal.

    _____

    _____

    _____

P A R T

4

Appendix

ANSWERS TO EXERCISES

EXERCISE: Test Your Knowledge (page 5)

1.   F   If you are not sure of your status, copies of local, state and federal laws can be obtained from the appropriate government agencies.

2.   F   Affirmative action means going beyond compliance with the law and includes taking assertive steps to ensure equal representation of women and minorities at all levels within an organization.

3.   T   Nothing in the equal opportunity laws requires the hiring or promotion of unqualified people.

4.   F   You should be concerned only with her qualifications for the job. The other concerns are assumptions without basis in fact.

5.   T   Performance is the name of the game.

6.   T   The regulations require "reasonable accommodation," which is determined partly on the basis of "financial cost and expenses" and "business necessity."

7.   T   Equal pay for equal work has nothing to do with outside income.

8.   F   Such behavior may be demoralizing, embarrassing and even threatening to some employees. Managers who permit or engage in this practice create a negative work climate for employees.

9.   F   This question violates federal, state and many city laws. This question has been ruled inappropriate by most compliance agencies. Statistics indicate minorities have been arrested (but not necessarily convicted) more than non-minorities, therefore, it could have an adverse impact on minority applicants.

10.   T   The Equal Employment Opportunity Act of 1972 enabled the Equal Employment Opportunity Commission (EEOC) to enforce Title VII in covered organizations through court action.

EXERCISE: Reading Review (page 61)

1. F The records are full of supporting reasons for this legislation.

2. F History speaks for itself.

3. F Imagination aside, minorities often have good grounds for charging discrimination.

4. T

5. T

6. T

7. T

8. F Tests must meet rigorous standards before they can be used in making personnel decisions.

9. T Family care absences include time to care for a newborn by both mother or father.

10. F The ADA law requires employers to make reasonable accommodations for disabled employees.

11. T

12. T

13. F If you answered true, you need to re-read this book.

14. T

15. F EEO is still either not accepted, not understood, or is ignored by a number of organizations.

ANSWERS TO CASE STUDIES

Solution to Case Study #1 (page 18)

Martin selected Rick Anderson.

If you made the same selection Martin did, you are in violation of the law!

He was afraid that if Rick didn't get the job he would leave the company. Martin liked Rick's ideas and besides, Rick was part of Martin's Saturday golfing foursome. Martin felt Rick was qualified based on his prior experience. He was sure Rick could develop adequate supervisory skills. In addition, Rick is young enough to have a long career once he learns to set some goals and accept company politics.

Martin considered Adele for the position but was concerned that as a woman, management wouldn't listen to her ideas. Besides, with children in college, Adele might marry again and lose all interest in a career.

Fred accepted the decision because he felt it was because he didn't qualify due to a lack of formal education. Fred also felt Rick wouldn't last long and that he would have a degree when the job opened up again.

Adele felt equal employment opportunity laws had been violated. She filed suit against the company. She felt she was discriminated against because of her age and gender. There were no women in management and Adele felt compelled to assert herself to get affirmative action started in the company. Her action brought the EEOC in direct contact with the underutilization of women in supervisory and management positions in the company.

Adele won her case and was promoted to supervisor. In addition, because of her action, the company has been directed to design and implement an acceptable affirmative action plan.

Solution to Case Study #2 (page 26)

How did this situation get started?
Sam Green's reasons for treating Karen, (and other women) in the office as he does is a matter for speculation. His values and Eileen's too may come from role modeling that perpetuates discrimination against women, or that men are supposed to treat secretaries and clericals that way. Regardless, he will never know that Karen doesn't like his behavior unless she tells him.

What could be done to prevent this situation?

Training on affirmative action and sexual harassment should have been provided for all managers and supervisors, including Sam Green and Eileen Berk. Neither obviously understood the equal employment opportunity laws. Sam should be a proper role model for Eileen. The workmen should have been made aware that jokes, whistles, comments, touching or lewd looks are inappropriate. In a typically male work environment, management should address the issue of sexual harassment and take steps to reinforce proper behavior.

It is also important for supervisors and managers to look at the other side of the issue and reinforce proper dress codes. Men and women who wear tight or revealing garments, or do not wear undergarments, can be inviting sexual harassment. Further, flirtatious behavior can be construed as sexual harassment if it is unwanted or bothers someone.

How could the harassment have been stopped?

Karen should have told Sam Green that his comments and touching made her uncomfortable. She should have also reported the whistling, offensive jokes, and lewd behavior to Sam Green. If it was not stopped, she should have called the Personnel Department directly.

Karen should have documented each incident by keeping a log including the date, place, remark, and any witnesses present.

How can this situation be resolved?

Karen should reconstruct all the incidents that have occurred to date and document them. She should then make Sam Green and the Personnel Department aware of all the incidents and the anguish it all causes her. If there is no improvement she should seek legal counsel.

In addition, Hercules Tire needs to examine its position under the law and take affirmative action to prevent sexual harassment in the future.

Solution to Case Study #3 (page 55)

Bill Williams is not the first supervisor to make this series of mistakes, but he could be the last if managers paid more attention to the basic requirements of good supervision.

Bill should have established measurable performance standards for each of his employees and worked with them to keep the standards current at all times. Each new employee should have been introduced to the expected standards and given a reasonable time to achieve proficiency.

The performance of employees who could not achieve the standards, (or chose not to), should have been reviewed with them periodically and documented. Corrective steps should have been placed in writing and monitored for results. If termination resulted, the reason should have been clearly documented and mutually understood. The performance of the employees meeting standards should also have been reviewed periodically and their achievement reinforced.

Reuben probably was not discriminated against because of race, but Bill's approach left it open to question. Chances are a court would have ruled in Reuben's favor.

GLOSSARY OF TERMS

ADA
The Americans with Disabilities Act of 1990. Title I of the ADA, which prohibits discrimination in hiring, took effect for companies with 15 or more employees on July 26, 1994. It covers all employers, including state and federal agencies, except private clubs and religious organizations. The ADA is a "nondiscrimination" law rather than an "affirmative action" one. It has no recruiting requirements. It does require that organizations look first at a person's abilities rather than automatically excluding them on the basis of perceived inability resulting from a disability.

AFFIRMATIVE ACTION
Commitment to achieving the intent of equal opportunity legislation through a detailed set of objectives and plans designed to achieve prompt and full utilization of minorities, women, handicapped persons and Vietnam-era veterans at all levels and in all areas of the workforce.

DISCRIMINATION
Showing some favoritism or partiality in the treatment of employees as compared to others.

DISPARATE TREATMENT
Treating an employee of another race, religion, sex, color, or national origin differently.

EEOC
Equal Employment Opportunity Commission, which handles complaints, investigations, and legal action on behalf of employees.

HANDICAPPED
Individuals who have a physical or mental impairment that limits one or more major life activities. One who has a record of, or is known to have, such an impairment.

MINORITY
A person having origins in Black racial groups of Africa, Mexican, Puerto Rican, Cuban, Central or South American or other Spanish culture or origin regardless of race, Asians, Pacific Islanders, Native Americans or Alaskan Natives.

PROTECTED CLASS
Women and men over the age of 40.

REVERSE DISCRIMINATION
Hiring, promoting, training or retaining unqualified or non-performing minorities over white males.

SEXUAL HARASSMENT	Deliberate or repeated, unsolicited verbal comments, gestures or physical contact of a sexual nature, which are unwelcome.
UNDERUTILIZATION	Having fewer minorities or women in a particular job group than would reasonably be expected by their availability in the job market.
VETERANS	Disabled veterans are persons entitled to compensation for a disability incurred or aggravated in the line of duty, which caused release or discharge from active duty.
	Qualified disabled veterans are disabled veterans capable of performing a particular job, with reasonable accommodations for the disability.
	Vietnam veterans are persons who served on active duty for more than 180 days during the Vietnam Era and were discharged or released with other than a dishonorable discharge, or were discharged or released due to a disability that was incurred during the Vietnam Era.
VRR	The Veteran's Reemployment Rights (VRR) Law. A relatively new statute signed by President Clinton on October 13, 1994 expanding the rights of service men and women who return to the workforce after a period of military service.

REFERENCES

Affirmative Action. H. W. Wilson: NY, NY. 1991.

A reference book that contains articles that describe the legal aspects of affirmative action, prospects of affirmative action in the workplace, the attitudes of whites toward affirmative action, and reflections of a diverse group on how affirmative action has affected their lives.

A Conflict of Rights. Melvin I. Urofsky. Scribner's Sons: NY, NY.

A dramatic and human story about a woman who got a job while fearing the "old boy network" would keep her out and a man who felt discriminated against when he didn't get the job. It discusses the right to be hired and crucial Supreme Court cases.

Debating Affirmative Action. Nicolaus Mills. Dell Publishing (Bantam-Doubleday-Dell): NY, NY. 1994.

Overviews feminism and affirmative action, equality and identity. It outlines goals, timetables, the glass ceiling, racial preference, the great white myth and the choices we have for real equal opportunity.

Landmark Decisions of the United States Supreme Court. Excellent Books: Beverly Hills, California. 1991.

A majority opinion of the court as expressed by the Justice chosen to speak for the court.

The New Leaders. Ann Morrison. Jossey-Bass: San Francisco, California. 1992.

Reveals "best practices" for promoting white women and people of color, and offers a step-by-step action plan for creating diversity strategies that achieve measurable results. It contains specific recruitment development and accountability tools that foster diversity and help organizations compete effectively for the best management employees available.

Paved with Good Intentions. Jared Taylor. Carroll & Graf Publishers, Inc.: NY, NY. 1992.

Explores why we have failed to accomplish goals of the civil rights movement. Explores the gap between beliefs and public discussion, racism, double standards and what can be done.

Racism and Justice. Gertrude Ezorsky. Cornell University Press: Ithaca, New York. 1991.

Focus is on black persons as beneficiaries of affirmative action in employment and their unique entitlement to special efforts to ensure the fair share of employment benefits.

Reflections of An Affirmative Action Baby. Stephen L. Carter. Basic Books: NY, NY. 1991.

Using his own story and frustrations, the author provides an analysis of the pressures on black professionals and intellectuals to conform to one "politically correct" way of being black. He argues that affirmative action as practiced today fails to promote equality and escapes our moral obligation.

Sexual Harassment. Lynne Eisaguirre. ABC-CLIO, Inc.: Santa Barbara, California. 1993.

An overview of laws, facts and statistics, with surveys of incidences among groups and professionals.

BIBLIOGRAPHY

Books

Smart Hiring: The Complete Guide to Hiring Employees
Robert Wendover, 1989
Management Staff Press, Inc.
7500 E. Arapahoe Road
Englewood, Colorado 80112
(800) 227-5510

Labor and Employment Law:
Compliance and Litigation
Frederick T. Golder, 1987
Callaghan & Company
3201 Old Glenview Road
Wilmette, IL 60091

The Law of the Workplace:
Rights of Employers and Employees
Frederick T. Golder, 1987
Callaghan & Company
3201 Old Glenview Road
Wilmette, IL 60091

Employment Law in the 50 States:
A Reference for Employees
CUE/NAM
1331 Pennsylvania Avenue, NW
Suite 1500–North Lobby
Washington, DC 20004-1703

Supervising Employees with Disabilities
Mary B. Dickson, 1993
Crisp Publications, Inc.
Menlo Park, CA

Job Hunting Tips for the So-Called Handicapped or People Who Have Disabilities
Richard Nelson Bolles, 1991
Ten Speed Press
Berkeley, CA

Americans with Disabilities Act Technical Assistance Manual
Prepared jointly by the Equal Employment Opportunity Commission and the Justice Department
U.S. Government Printing Office

Quality Interviewing, Third Edition
Robert B. Maddux, 1994
Crisp Publications, Inc.
Menlo Park, CA

Periodicals

HR Magazine
Society for Human Resource Management
606 N. Washington Street
Alexandria, VA 22314
(703) 548-3440

HR News
Society for Human Resource Management
606 N. Washington Street
Alexandria, VA 22314
(703) 548-3440

Personnel Journal
P.O. Box 2440
Costa Mesa, CA 92628
(714) 751-1883

Employment Practice Reference Sources
Bureau of National Affairs
1231 25th Street NW
Washington, DC 20037
(301) 258-1033

Bureau of Law and Business
64 Wall Street
Madison, CT 06443
(800) 553-4569

EEOC
Publications Department
2401 E Street, NW
Washington, DC 20507
(202) 634-6922

Assessment

GUIDE TO AFFIRMATIVE ACTION— REVISED EDITION

GUIDE TO AFFIRMATIVE ACTION
REVISED EDITION

A FIFTY-MINUTE™ BOOK

The objectives of this book are:

1. to explain Equal Employment Opportunity Commission (EEOC) legislation.

2. to point out EEOC responsibilities of management to employees.

3. to clarify management hiring and layoff responsibilities.

OBJECTIVE ASSESSMENT FOR GUIDE TO AFFIRMATIVE ACTION

Select the best response.

1. If you must lay off one employee, you should select the one with the poorest performance record regardless of age, race, religion, sex, handicap or veteran's status.
   A. True
   B. False

2. It is perfectly legal to ask applicants if they have ever been arrested.
   A. True
   B. False

3. The equal pay act of 1963 requires that
   A. men and women must receive equal pay for substantially similar jobs.
   B. seniority systems cannot exist.
   C. business factors other than sex cannot affect hiring decisions.
   D. all of the above.

4. The Rehabilitation Act of 1973
   A. bans discrimination of handicapped individuals.
   B. requires that mental illness be considered a covered handicap.
   C. requires that handicaps must substantially limit one or more major life activity.
   D. requires that companies actively hire and support handicapped individuals.
   E. all of the above.

5. The Family and Medical Leave Act of 1993
   A. permits 12 weeks of unpaid leave for medical or serious family health problems.
   B. limits pregnancy leave to females.
   C. allows leave to be taken as often as needed.
   D. all of the above.

6. It is unlawful to use any screening technique for employment that cannot be proved to be directly job related.
   A. True
   B. False

OBJECTIVE ASSESSMENT (continued)

7. A detailed and company-specific affirmative action plan in writing is required of
   A. all United States companies that pay wages.
   B. federal contractors and subcontractors with 50 or more employees and over $50,000 in contracts.
   C. all United States companies employing labor overseas.
   D. all of the above.

8. Age discrimination laws
   A. apply to people between 40 and 70 years of age by federal law.
   B. protect all ages in some states.
   C. apply to all employees of companies receiving federal money.
   D. all of the above.
   E. A and C.

9. Which could be considered sexual harassment?
   A. A person tells a joke about blondes, women or homosexuals.
   B. An employee is annoyed by a friendly gesture or touch by another employee.
   C. A female worker wears provocative clothing at work.
   D. all of the above.
   E. B and C.

10. Organizations are required to communicate EEOC policy both internally and externally.
    A. True
    B. False

11. An acceptable affirmative action program must include
    A. an analysis of the current workforce to determine sex and race composition.
    B. identification of deficiencies.
    C. written goals, timetables and audits.
    D. all of the above.
    E. A and B.

12. White males may have a significant advantage in an organization if
    A. all key decision makers are white males.
    B. white males tend to associate exclusively with other white males.
    C. white males get promoted more frequently than women or minorities.
    D. any of the above.

13. To enforce EEOC policy, organizations must have
    A. in place measurable standards of performance for management regarding EEOC responsibilities.
    B. disciplinary systems based on performance against EEOC standards.
    C. job specifications based on bona fide job requirements.
    D. fair hiring and promotional practices.
    E. all of the above.

14. If you believe that women can't compete at the executive levels of your company
    A. you still must hire them, regardless of their experience, for executive positions.
    B. you are in danger of a Title VII violation.
    C. your company will probably suffer if you take a chance on them.
    D. any of the above.

15. Which of the following is true?
    A. People without a high school diploma cannot read adequately.
    B. Women have a higher turnover rate than men have.
    C. White people are generally more intelligent than Blacks or Hispanics.
    D. All of the above.
    E. None of the above.

16. Employers will have success with EEOC goals if
    A. they have no personal biases.
    B. they are proactive with EEOC company policies.
    C. if adequate EEOC regulations are written and publicized.
    D. all of the above.
    E. B and C.

17. Anyone with a physical handicap will not be able to produce as much as someone can who does not have a handicap.
    A. True
    B. False

18. Goals
    A. are expressed quantitatively.
    B. are statements of results which are to be achieved.
    C. should be challenging but achievable.
    D. all of the above.
    E. B and C.

OBJECTIVE ASSESSMENT (continued)

19. To continue practices that perpetuate discrimination is illegal whether done consciously or unconsciously.
    A. True
    B. False

20. Disabled employees
    A. must have special equipment if needed.
    B. may have specialized job descriptions.
    C. both of the above.
    D. neither of the above.

21. Anyone involved in hiring
    A. has certain prejudices. C
    B. must know local as well as federal EEOC laws.
    C. must use performance based criteria.
    D. all of the above.
    E. B and C.

22. A standard is
    A. a goal.
    B. usually expressed quantitatively.
    C. more common for repetitive task workers than for managers.
    D. all of the above.
    E. B and C.

23. The job appraisal discussion should
    A. emphasize questions with *yes* or *no* answers. B. include an action plan with timetable.
    C. involve employee decision making.
    D. all of the above.
    E. B and C.

24. It is O.K. to use paper and pencil tests to screen applicants if these instruments can help with a hiring decision.
    A. True
    B. False

25. The Americans with Disabilities Act of 1990
    A. prohibits discrimination in hiring.
    B. includes private clubs and religious organizations.
    C. has specific recruiting requirements.
    D. all of the above.
    E. A and B.

Qualitative Objectives for *Guide to Affirmative Action—Revised Edition*

To explain Equal Employment Opportunity (EEOC) legislation

Questions 3, 4, 5, 8, 9, 25

To point out EEOC responsibilities of management

Questions 7, 10, 11, 12, 13, 14, 15, 16, 17, 18, 19, 22, 23

To clarify management hiring and layoff responsibilities

Questions 1, 2, 6, 20, 21, 24

ANSWER KEY

1. A	**10.** A	**18.** E
2. B	**11.** D	**19.** A
3. A	**12.** D	**20.** C
4. E	**13.** E	**21.** D
5. A	**14.** B	**22.** E
6. A	**15.** E	**23.** E
7. B	**16.** B	**24.** B
8. D	**17.** B	**25.** A
9. D		

NOTES

NOW AVAILABLE FROM
CRISP PUBLICATIONS

Books • Videos • CD Roms • Computer-Based Training Products

If you enjoyed this book, we have great news for you. There are over 200 books available in the *50-Minute*™ Series. To request a free full-line catalog, contact your local distributor or Crisp Publications, Inc., 1200 Hamilton Court, Menlo Park, CA 94025. Our toll-free number is 800-442-7477.

Subject Areas Include:

Management

Human Resources

Communication Skills

Personal Development

Marketing/Sales

Organizational Development

Customer Service/Quality

Computer Skills

Small Business and Entrepreneurship

Adult Literacy and Learning

Life Planning and Retirement

CRISP WORLDWIDE DISTRIBUTION

English language books are distributed worldwide. Major international distributors include:

ASIA/PACIFIC

Australia/New Zealand: In Learning, PO Box 1051, Springwood QLD, Brisbane, Australia 4127   Tel: 61-7-3-841-2286, Facsimile: 61-7-3-841-1580
ATTN: Messrs. Gordon

Singapore: 85, Genting Lane, Guan Hua Warehouse Bldng #05-01, Singapore 349569   Tel: 65-749-3389, Facsimile: 65-749-1129
ATTN: Evelyn Lee

Japan: Phoenix Associates Co., LTD., Mizuho Bldng. 3-F, 2-12-2, Kami Osaki, Shinagawa-Ku, Tokyo 141   Tel: 81-33-443-7231, Facsimile: 81-33-443-7640
ATTN: Mr. Peter Owans

CANADA

Reid Publishing, Ltd., Box 69559-109 Thomas Street, Oakville, Ontario Canada L6J 7R4.   Tel: (905) 842-4428, Facsimile: (905) 842-9327
ATTN: Mr. Stanley Reid

Trade Book Stores: *Raincoast Books*, 8680 Cambie Street, Vancouver, B.C., V6P 6M9   Tel: (604) 323-7100, Facsimile: (604) 323-2600
ATTN: Order Desk

EUROPEAN UNION

England: *Flex Training*, Ltd. 9-15 Hitchin Street, Baldock, Hertfordshire, SG7 6A, England   Tel: 44-1-46-289-6000, Facsimile: 44-1-46-289-2417
ATTN: Mr. David Willetts

INDIA

Multi-Media HRD, Pvt., Ltd., National House, Tulloch Road, Appolo Bunder, Bombay, India 400-039   Tel: 91-22-204-2281, Facsimile: 91-22-283-6478
ATTN: Messrs. Aggarwal

SOUTH AMERICA

Mexico: *Grupo Editorial Iberoamerica*, Nebraska 199, Col. Napoles, 03810 Mexico, D.F.   Tel: 525-523-0994, Facsimile: 525-543-1173
ATTN: Señor Nicholas Grepe

SOUTH AFRICA

Alternative Books, Unit A3 Micro Industrial Park, Hammer Avenue, Stridom Park, Randburg, 2194 South Africa   Tel: 27-11-792-7730, Facsimile: 27-11-792-7787
ATTN: Mr. Vernon de Haas